Bebop
JAZZ GUITAR

HEAD TRANSCRIPTIONS AND FULL BACKING
TRACKS FOR 12 CLASSICS

BY SHAWN PERSINGER

ISBN 978-1-4234-9402-7

HAL•LEONARD®
CORPORATION
7777 W. BLUEMOUND RD. P.O. BOX 13819 MILWAUKEE, WI 53213

Visit Hal Leonard Online at
www.halleonard.com

PAGE		CD TRACK
4	PREFACE	
5	MAJOR SCALE PATTERNS	
6	CHORD DIAGRAMS	
7	ANTHROPOLOGY	1
8	BE-BOP	2
10	BOPLICITY (BE BOP LIVES)	3
12	CONCEPTION	4
14	CONFIRMATION	5
13	DANCE OF THE INFIDELS	6
16	DONNA LEE	7
18	GROOVIN' HIGH	8
19	HALF NELSON	9
20	SHAWNUFF	10
22	TEMPUS FUGIT	11
21	WELL YOU NEEDN'T (IT'S OVER NOW)	12
24	ABOUT THE AUTHOR	
	TUNING NOTES	13

PREFACE

FINGERINGS AND ARTICULATION: PRACTICE SUGGESTIONS

Frequently, tunes written for the saxophone or trumpet during the bebop era do not translate easily to comfortable fingering positions on the guitar. Typically, the rapid modulations (key changes) that occur in bebop tunes move to keys that are not "guitar-friendly." Tunes like "Anthropology" and "Shawnuff" adapt with little trouble to the guitar because those particular tunes exist in a, more or less, static key center. But songs such as "Half Nelson" and "Groovin' High" have a quick progression of key changes that can make fingerings for the guitar awkward. Choosing the "best" fingerings for these melodies was done through much experimentation and refinement. These fingerings should not be considered definitive but they should be comfortable for most guitarists. With that being said, I encourage you to try alternate fingerings and articulations.

I suggest that you pencil in rhythmic stems and rests where needed in the tablature. Unless you already have an intimate relationship with these particular songs, the syncopated, varied, and purposely confusing rhythms can be quite difficult for many players to navigate. A phrase at first glance might appear to be a triplet, but could, in fact, be two sixteenths followed by a quarter note. Do not take these subtle differences for granted; they can have a huge musical impact when playing with other musicians. I chose not to insert rhythms into the tablature because it can clutter and confuse some players. My final decision was to leave them out because you, the reader/player, can always write them in yourself, but you would not have been able to erase them if they were included.

One final note concerning the fingerings: I chose to vary the octave registers the tunes are played in. My decision to do this was at times arbitrary, but I went with what felt and sounded best. I also believe that mixing up the registers encourages superior utilization of the entire fretboard.

MAJOR SCALE PATTERNS

On the following page there are the five major scale patterns (with their modal names) I—and, I believe, most guitarists—use most often. I have included and referenced them for each tune so players will know what positions they are playing in and around.

CHORD DIAGRAMS

The chord shapes used in this book, like the fingerings, were chosen because of their multifunctional applications in jazz standards and the fact that they constitute the most basic, essential, and well-known jazz chord shapes. Like the fingerings, though, they are only suggestions. Often, the chords I've chosen do not lend themselves to smooth voice leading, something many chord-melody players hold sacrosanct. As a result, I've tried to vary the shapes from tune to tune, and you should feel free to mix and match them.

The Chord Diagrams section demonstrates alternate voicings, fingerings, and substitutions for several common chords.

MAJOR SCALE PATTERNS

Shown in the key of G major (E minor) with their modal pattern names. Root notes are circled.

Pattern 1: Ionian (major)

Pattern 2: Dorian

Pattern 3: Phrygian

Pattern 4: Mixolydian

Pattern 5: Aeolian (natural minor)

CHORD DIAGRAMS
Alternative Voicings, Fingerings, and Substitutions

An "o" over an unfretted string means to play it open. An "x" over an unfretted string means to not play it.

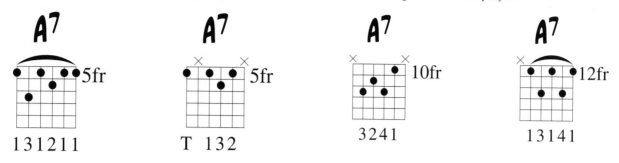

Ninth and 13th chords often, but not always, work as jazzier alternatives to 7th chords. Use your ear to judge the situation.

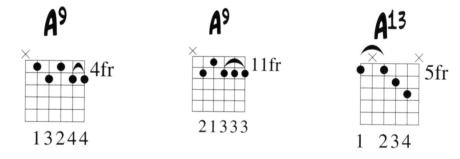

A 7♭5 chord is the same as a 7♯11 chord. A 7♯5 is the same as a 7♭13. Theoretically the ♭5/♯11 and ♯5/♭13 are in different octaves, but in practice they are interchangeable.

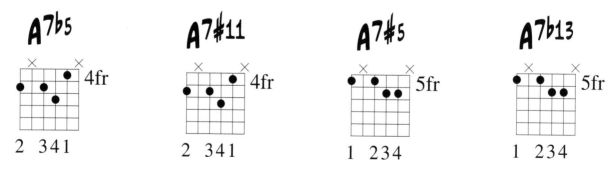

ANTHROPOLOGY

By Charlie Parker and Dizzy Gillespie

7

Position Notes: Intro played primarily out of
the 3rd position, Phrygian pattern, starting
at the 8th fret. A section primarily out of the
4th position, Mixolydian pattern starting at
the 11th fret.

Be-Bop

By John "Dizzy" Gillespie

TRACK 02

Intro
Fast (♪♪ = ♪³♪)

8

Boplicity
(Be Bop Lives)
By Miles Davis and Gil Evans

TRACK 03

A

MEDIUM SWING

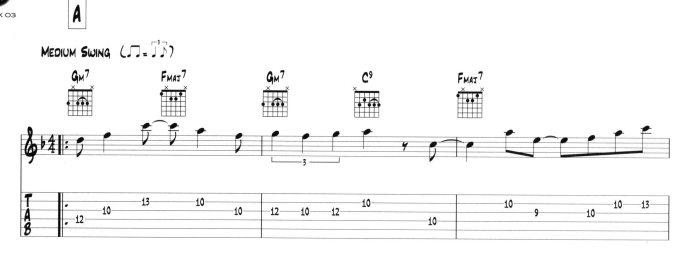

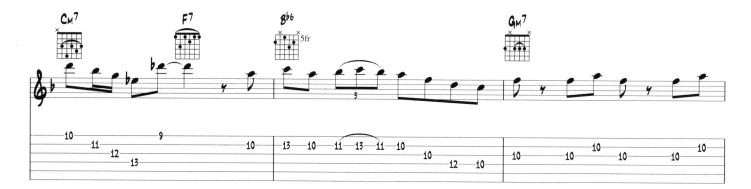

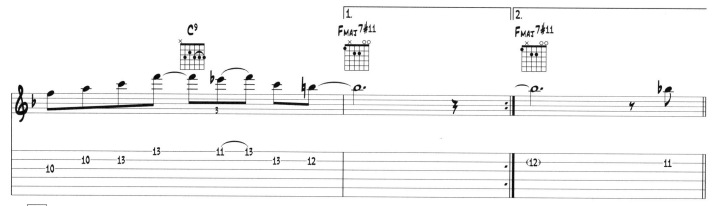

B

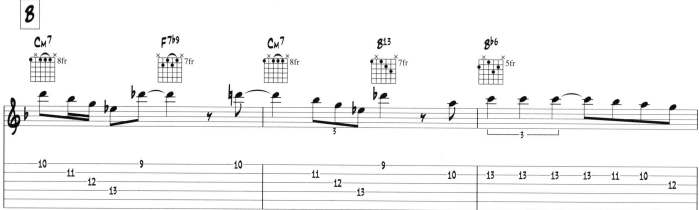

Conception

By George Shearing

Position Notes: [A] section played primarily out of the 1st position, Ionian pattern starting at the 9th fret.

TRACK 04

Dance of the Infidels

By Earl "Bud" Powell

Position Notes: A section played primarily out of the 5th position, Aeolian pattern at the 10th fret.

Confirmation

By Charlie Parker

TRACK 05

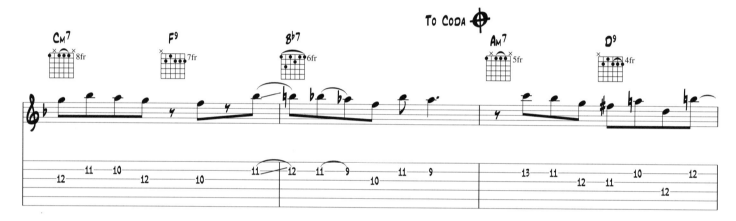

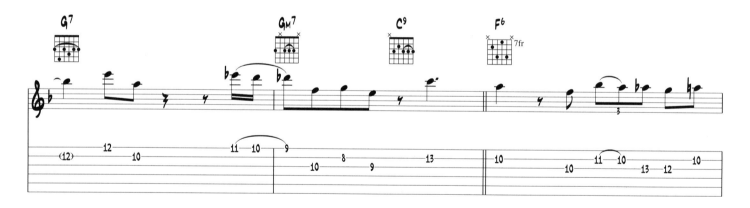

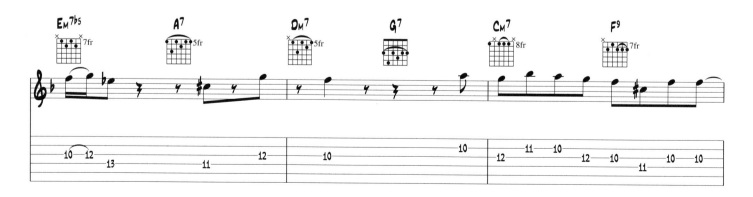

D.C. AL CODA

Donna Lee

By Charlie Parker

Position Notes: Starts out of the 3rd-position, Phrygian pattern starting at the 8th fret, but this one moves around quite a bit—very challenging.

Fast Swing

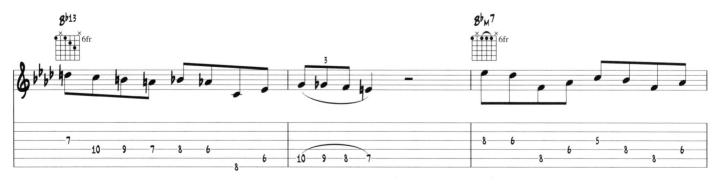

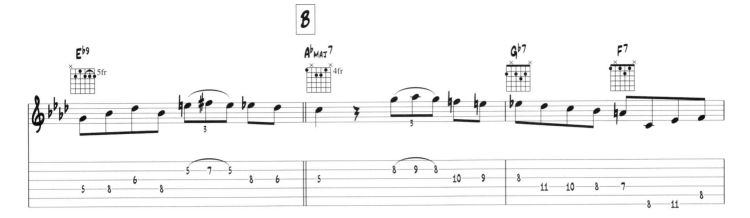

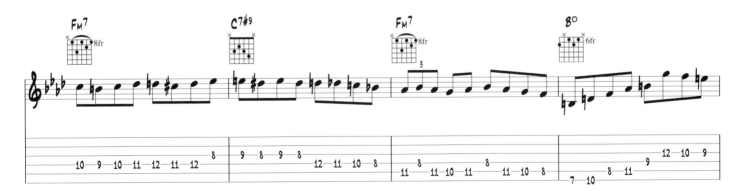

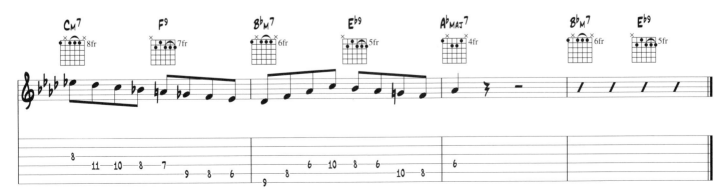

Groovin' High

By John "Dizzy" Gillespie

Half Nelson

By Miles Davis

TRACK 09

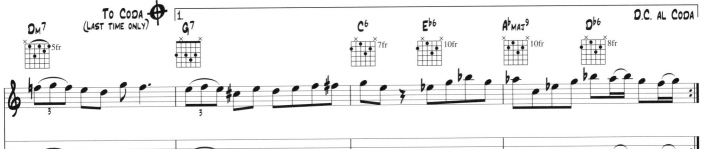

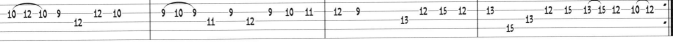

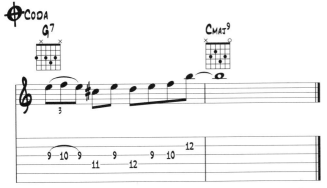

Shawnuff

By Charlie Parker and John "Dizzy" Gillespie

Position Notes: Played primarily out of the 3rd-position, Phrygian pattern starting at the 10th fret.

TRACK 10

20

Position Notes: This melody is not based out of a scale pattern. Rather it is based on arpeggios that correspond to the chords.

Well You Needn't
(It's Over Now)

Words by Mike Ferro
Music by Thelonious Monk

TRACK 12

A 𝄋

Medium Swing

B

D.S. al Coda

Position Notes: Played primarily out of the 3rd-position, Phrygian pattern starting at the 5th fret.

TEMPUS FUGIT

By Earl "Bud" Powell

TRACK 11

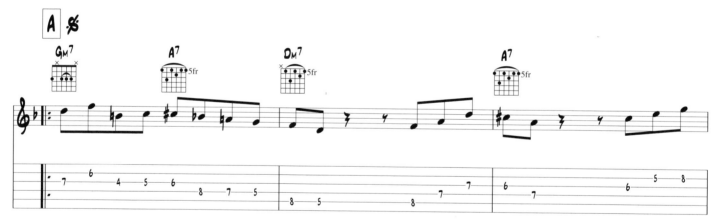

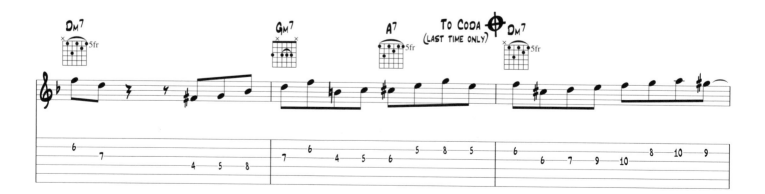

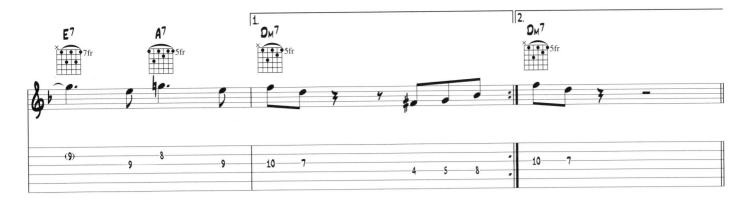

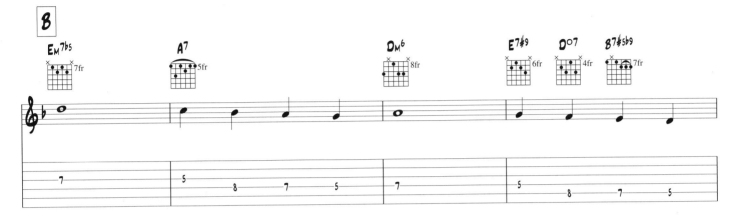

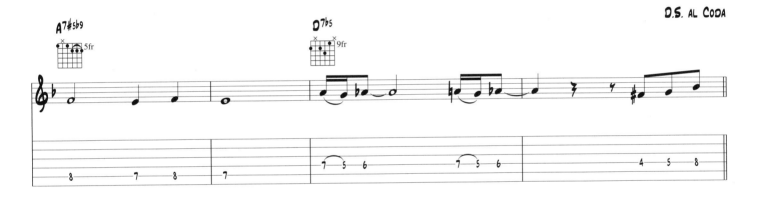

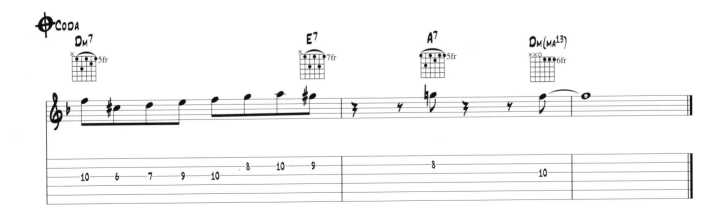

23

ABOUT THE AUTHOR

PHOTO BY KIVA SUTTON

Shawn Persinger is one of the most innovative composers, guitarists and singer/songwriters writing, teaching, and performing today. Drawing on a wealth of influences, Shawn has combined the best of classical, rock, jazz, folk, world music, and the avant-garde to develop a sound that is uniquely his own.

From his solo guitar music to his work with the groundbreaking avant-rock band, Boud Deun, his pieces for the "concert" music world to his aggressive folksinger style, Shawn has proven that his musical sensibility is unlimited. His latest project, Prester John, is being hailed as one of the most forward-thinking outfits to hit the acoustic music scene in years. The press and public agree: praise for his playing ability and composition style by publications as far-reaching as *Rolling Stone*, *The Washington Post*, *The Village Voice*, *Guitar World* and many others has helped Shawn gain worldwide recognition.

Shawn graduated from Musicians Institute in Los Angeles, CA in 1991, and has had a nineteen-year professional music career as a composer, performer and teacher. As a composer and performer Shawn has had his music publicly performed in varying ensembles, on five continents, in 36 countries and countless cities. He continues to tour and perform constantly around the world.

As a music educator, Shawn has taught thousands of students and instructed and directed multifarious ensembles and group workshops. He has also written articles, features and lessons for *Guitar Player* magazine, *Frets* and Taylor Guitar's *Wood & Steel*. Shawn is currently a faculty member of Guitar Intensives in Bar Harbor, ME, The Center for Creative Youth in Middletown, CT, and has also served on the faculty at The National Guitar Workshop.

To learn more about Shawn Persinger, his music, and his writing please visit **www.PersingerMusic.com**.